M… s Notebook

and Other Kinds of Writing

compiled by Brian Moses

Oxford University Press 1994

Oxford University Press, Walton Street, Oxford OX2 6DP

Oxford New York Toronto
Delhi Bombay Calcutta Madras Karachi
Kuala Lumpur Singapore Hong Kong Tokyo
Nairobi Dar es Salaam Cape Town
Melbourne Auckland Madrid

and associate companies in
Berlin Ibadan

Oxford is a trade mark of Oxford University Press

Published by Oxford University Press 1994

A CIP catalogue record for this book is available from the British Library

ISBN 0 19 916615 3

Typeset by Pentacor PLC, High Wycombe

Printed and bound in Hong Kong

Contents

Forty-Three Ways to be Happy

Roger Stevens

Wake up in the morning and smile. Laugh at Dad's jokes. Buy your Mum a present. Tell her you love her. Secretly tidy your bedroom. Stop thinking about the bad things you did yesterday; think of all the good things you've done. Buy yourself a present to celebrate something. Cook the dinner. Stroke the cat. Walk the dog. Smile lots. Sing a song. Learn your seven times table. Let Auntie Mabel give you a kiss – and don't screw up your face afterwards. Say thank you and mean it. Don't tell tales. Read a book. Write a story. Draw a picture of your Dad smiling. Help an old lady across the road. Make a resolution and keep it. Pretend it's your birthday. Decide what you want to be when you grow up. Make your own list of good things. Play football. Learn to juggle. Plant

some seeds. Keep a secret. Be a good friend. Run an errand. Give all your money to Oxfam. Devise a machine to cure pollution. Get up early and go for a walk. Help your teacher. Learn a musical instrument. Stand on your head. Think of somebody that everyone admires, then try to be like him or her – pretty soon everyone will like you, too. Copy your Mum and Dad's best points. Write a poem. Write a letter to Father Christmas asking for a present for somebody else. Say a prayer for peace. Every morning tell yourself that today's going to be your best day ever. Decide to be the best that you can be. Who's in charge of your life anyway? You are. What you do is up to you.

Our Family's Taking Back Christmas Shopping List

Ian Souter

A winter coat
– too big, too colourful, too expensive

A pocket game
– wouldn't work, wouldn't fit into my pocket

A digital watch
– dead battery, dead beat

A radio-controlled car
– went out of control, went out of the window

A moving doll
– turned it on, head fell off, turned it off

A pair of shorts
– the elastic snapped, the trousers fell down

A hair dryer
– won't go, won't blow

A pair of tights
- kept snagging, kept sagging

A new perfume
- wrong sort, wrong pong

A plastic football
- one hard kick, one flat ball

A mountain bike
- brakes slammed on, brakes jammed on

A pair of socks
- too small, two left feet

And if Santa had been around we would
have taken him back

or on second thoughts perhaps we would
have given him the sack!

An A-Z of Items Found on the School Roof by the Caretaker

Wes Magee

Apple core (brown)
'Better English' book (spotted with ink)
Crisps (unopened bag)
Dead bird (a starling . . . I think)

Earwig (inside a matchbox)
Felt pens in a case (thirty!)
Golf ball
Handkerchief (dirty!)

Ink cartridge (full)
Jaguar (model car)
Key (rusty)
Lunch box (labelled Paul Starr)

Marble (a bluey)
Nose (a false one: red)
Orange (all shrivelled)
Pencil (chewed at one end: no lead)

Queen's crown (from 2J's play)
Ruler (broken: old design)
Sock (shocking pink)
Tennis ball (mine!)

Underpants (Y-fronts)
Valentine card (to 'Farida Good')
Wellington boot
Xylophone block (wood)

Yellow scarf (Norwich City)
Zombie (a rubber horror . . . not pretty!)

All
brought
down
from
the
school
roof
by
the
caretaker . . .

Twenty-six items
from A-Z.
'Now write a story,
three pages at least
mentioning
every item,'
my
teacher
said.

Alphabet Shoes

Ian Souter

My shoes

Are
Bumpy, comfy,
Dependable, easy going
Footwear.
Gracefully heeled,
Interesting,
Jumping kickers.
Leaky, muddy, niggly,
Or
Posh, quiet
Road-runners.
Squeezy, tight
Underfoot,
Very whiffy,
Xpensive,
Yet
Zoomy.

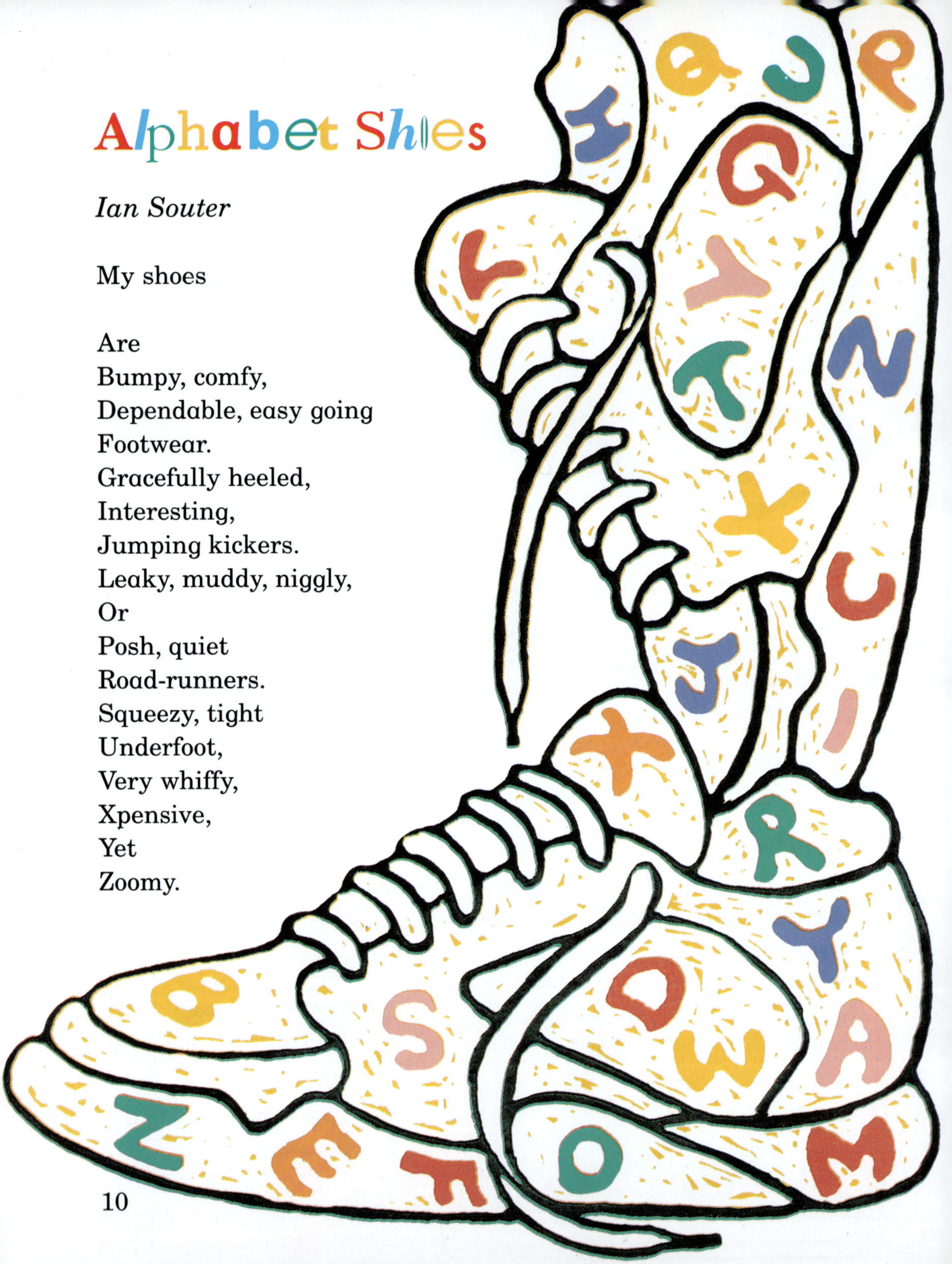

Messages

Pie Corbett

Message for the Mosquito Who Shares My Bedroom

I'm fed up with the way you keep me awake. You wait till I've just turned the light off and settled down for a good night's zizzzz before starting up your irritating whine. Announcing, 'Mister Mosquito is out for a bite.' At any second I expect to feel you puncture my skin and suck my blood. Tiny vampire, I am not your personal ketchup bottle. If I find you've settled nearby, I'll swat you flat. Be warned – go pester some other source of blood.

Message for the Mice that Live in the Roof

I've left you a present. It's not much – just a chunk of cheddar that had gone hard, and some bacon rind. I couldn't find anything classier in the fridge and I didn't think that you'd care much for scraps of garlic bread. I've left the cheese on the red dish by the cat flap.

Note for the Nightmare I Have About falling Off a Tall Building

Sorry, but I won't be in till late and by then you should have gone to sleep. Don't stay up on my behalf. I'll grab myself a bite to eat – just something cold from the fridge. I'm buying myself a trapeze artist's net to catch my dreams.

Note for My Angry Feelings

Look, this just won't do. Every time you butt your head into what I'm doing you end up spoiling things. We're all fed up with your red hot current and your poisonous tongue. If you can't stay put then I'm in for real trouble. My Mum did not appreciate being told that she could be a stand-in for a dummy at an outsize clothes shop. So, button it.

Milk Notes in Story Street

Tony Mitton

A windy night has scattered all the milk notes in Story Street. Can you help the muddled milkman match them to the correct houses?

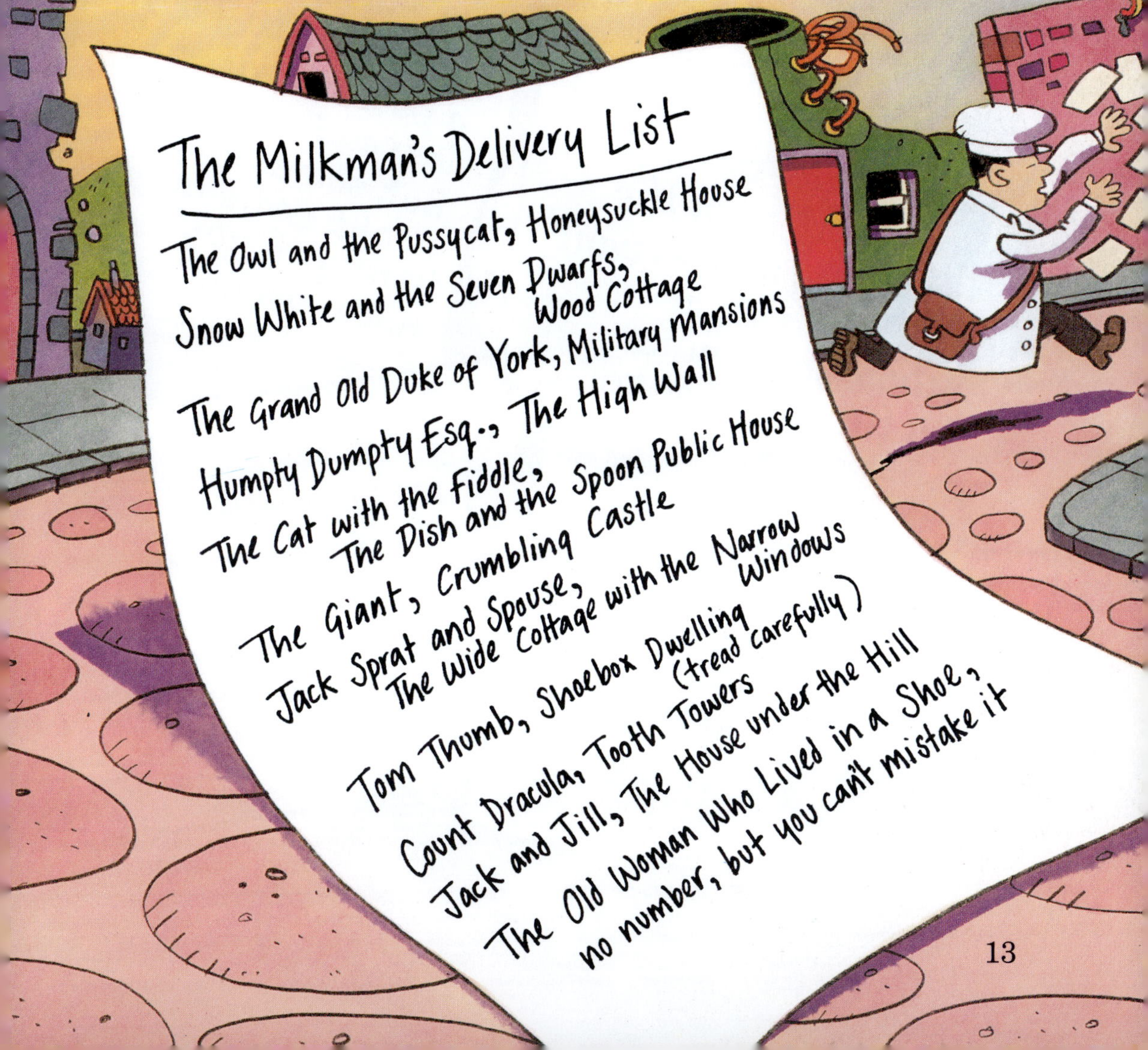

The Notes

7 half-pints and an apple yoghurt.

Milk! You must be joking! But leave me 3 pints of rhesus negative and a black pudding every night or you'll get it in the neck. My manservant will pay you in silver sovereigns by the great gate.

No milk today. We're off to fetch a pail of water instead. Sorry. But some vinegar might come in handy if you have any.

1 pint of double cream + 1 pint of skimmed milk (fat free) please. Find clean empties by front door. Thanks

Ten thousand and one pints of gold top, please. Leave deliveries on the top step, or the bottom step, or on the middle step (neither up nor down). The sentry will pay you each Saturday.

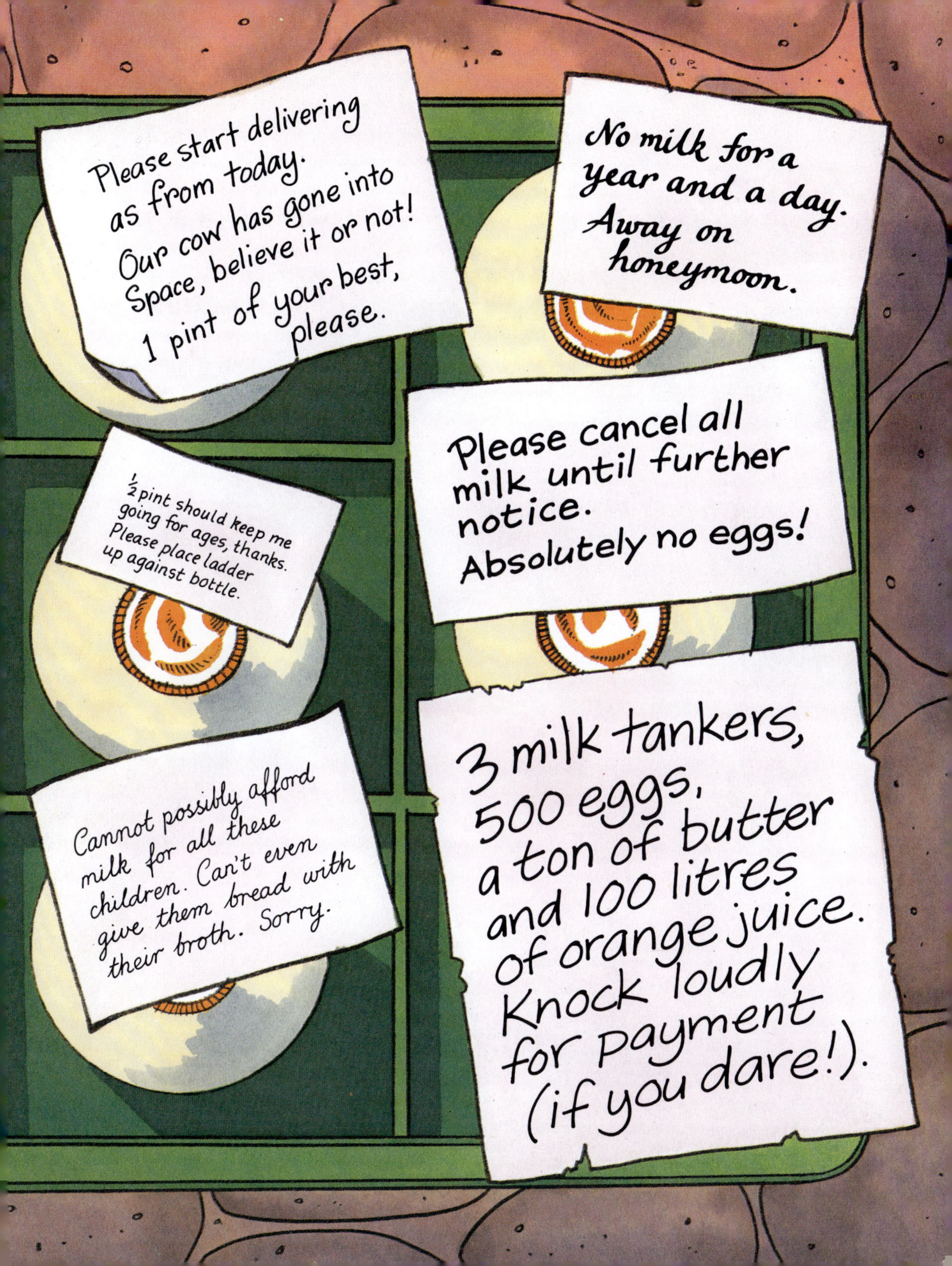
Please start delivering as from today. Our cow has gone into Space, believe it or not! 1 pint of your best, please.
No milk for a year and a day. Away on honeymoon.
½ pint should keep me going for ages, thanks. Please place ladder up against bottle.
Please cancel all milk until further notice. Absolutely no eggs!
Cannot possibly afford milk for all these children. Can't even give them bread with their broth. Sorry.
3 milk tankers, 500 eggs, a ton of butter and 100 litres of orange juice. Knock loudly for payment (if you dare!).

Recipe for Making Better

Gina Douthwaite

Ingredients
(things needed)
1 child
1 mangled bicycle
1 parent

Method (what to do)
1 Take a freshly twisted ankle and kiss away the pain.
2 Measure out sticking plaster and apply to blooded knee.
3 Add 1 medium-sized hug.
4 Melt several icy glares with a warm smile. Mix together.
5 Heat 2 small hands inside 2 larger ones.
6 Open 2 kind ears, and strain.
7 Fold in 1 extra large cuddle.
8 Sift in a good shake of laughter and a ruffle of hair.
9 Stir in 1 lifeful of love.
10 Pour into a pain-proof dish and simmer gently.

Menus

Robin Mellor

A Menu for the Iron Man

Starter

RUSTY NUTS AND BOLTS
IN A DELICIOUS SAUCE OF OLD ENGINE OIL
AND SPRINKLED WITH IRON FILINGS

Main Course

A COMPLETE OLD FACTORY BOILER
WITH CHOPPED GREASY STOVE
SLICED GIRDER AND CRUSHED CAR
SERVED WITH BARBED WIRE
IN A RUST REMOVER AND PAINT FLAKE GRAVY

Dessert

FRIED HUB-CAPS AND GROUND LAMP-POST

A BOTTLE OF PAINT STRIPPER TO ACCOMPANY
THE MEAL IS AVAILABLE AT EXTRA COST.

A Menu for Stig (of the Dump)

Starter

Nettle soup and chalk pit snails
cooked in an old tin can

Main Course

Squirrel pie with fried worms
garnished with delicious ants
boiled in a cracked teapot

Dessert

Blackberry, elderberry and rose-hip mousse
with hazelnut sauce and jam
from an old jam pot

To drink – rainwater collected in a can.

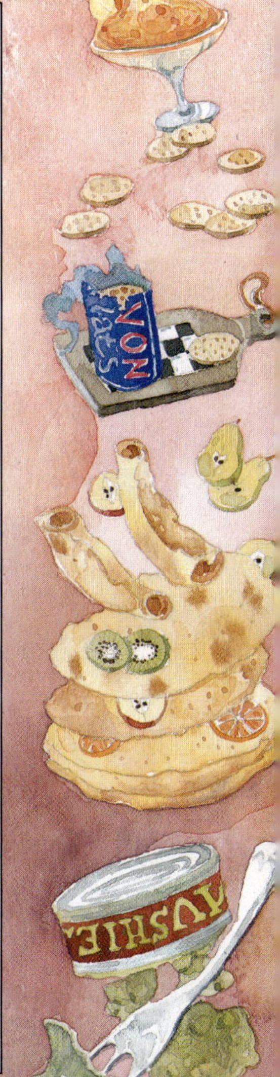

A Menu for Flat Stanley

Starter

PITTA BREAD AND SPAM SLICES

OR TODAY'S SPECIAL, SQUASHED TOMATO SOUP

Main Course

FRESH FLAT FISH AND PRESSED HAM

WITH EXTRA ROLLED PASTA AND MUSHY PEAS

IN A SQUISHY CHEESE SAUCE

Dessert

PANCAKES AND THIN SLICED FRUIT

WITH DEVON FLAT BISCUITS

A BOTTLE OF SQUASH IS AVAILABLE

AT EXTRA COST.

Travel Posters from Thomas Fox Travel Agents

Tony Mitton

MICE! FEELING TRAPPED?

Get away from that
dingy old mousehole.
Leave your cat behind.
Come to the Cheddar
Gorge and gorge
yourself on its gorgeous
local cheeses. Explore
its fascinating caverns,
homes of the giant mice
of long ago. Whisk
down to your nearest
branch of Thomas Fox
Travel Agents and sniff
out the facts. Cheese.
We aim to please.

Safari Hunting Holidays for cabin-crazy cats.

FELINE FRIENDS!

Come to the carefree Cheddar Gorge – mightiest mousetrap in the world. Rodents flock to its cheesy caves. Come hunting to your heart's content. More mice per mile says your Agent with the smile, Thomas Fox. Slink over for the info.

DOGS!

Bored with bones? Doped out on dog-food? Don't go barking mad.

Come to Cheddar for a fun-filled cat-chasing stray-away-day. Cheddar's caverns are crammed with cats. Bound from that basket to book a growlingly good holiday at your local branch of Thomas Fox. Get off that leash. Fetch, boy, fetch!

Mrs Noah's Notebook

Tony Mitton

As we shall be together on the Ark for some time, I have decided to open a little school. This should keep us all busy and help to pass the time. Who knows? Some of us may even learn something! I've decided to keep notes on the pupils' progress, just in case Mr Noah (or The Head himself) should ask about them.

Spiders
Very good at needlework. Also, keen goalkeepers (no flies on their catching). Beautifully crossed legs in assembly. Always follow the thread of the lesson exactly. Seem to have their projects all sewn up.

Flies

Not very good at settling to things, and therefore rather distracting to others. Keep up a constant buzz during lessons. (Perhaps we should have a quiet word about personal hygiene, handwashing, etc?)

Monkeys

A bit cheeky. Always chattering and mucking about in lessons. However, they're nimble gymnasts and very able on the apparatus. I wish they'd put their banana skins in the bin at breaktime.

Elephants

Very gentle, considering their size. A great help with stacking desks and chairs. Superb at remembering their spellings and tables.

Pigeons

Good at carrying messages around the Ark. But I wish they'd stop calling out 'COO!' in class all the time. And when will they start using the loos neatly?

Snails

Slow but steady workers. Rather shy at times and reluctant to come out of their shells. But they surprised us with some lovely dribble paintings. I think they might do well at calligraphy...

Hyenas

Seem to find everything very funny, which unsettles the rest of us. Don't join in much, and usually hang around at the edges of games and activities.

Frogs

Coming on in leaps and bounds. Very quiet and concentrated at times. Seem to enjoy the claywork and finger painting.

Ducks

Poor attendance. More interested in the outside world, really. Fair enough, considering...

Giraffes

They do look down on the others, I think. But then they are head and shoulders above the rest at most things.

Larks

What beautiful singers! They could rise to great heights in this area.

Cheetahs

Terrible copycats in class. But they knock spots off the others at deck-races.

Yetis

Serious concern here. Never turn up for register. Never attend classes. But occasional footprints near larder, and missing food, suggest they're here on board somewhere.

I must remember to keep these notes going. I'm sure they'll be useful for writing final reports. Still, time for hammock now. I can't help thinking what a pity it was that we couldn't get the dinosaurs aboard. But they were so very bulky (and let's face it – pea-brained).

Dinosaur Author

JONATHAN Shelly is Britain's youngest published author. At just four-and-a-half years old he has already written a book – about dinosaurs.

At first it was just a story which he told his parents to keep them amused on long car journeys, all about the dinosaurs' secret life. Eventually his mother wrote it down and turned it into a book.

Until recently his ambition was to be a dinosaur when he grew up but he has since changed his mind.

RUDE AWAKENING

A sleepwalker was shocked when he opened his eyes, to find himself locked out of his house, in Brighton, without any clothes on. A police inspector – called to the scene after the man was found entering the house by breaking a window – said he seemed to be 'very embarrassed'.

A fossil finding

A 230-million-year-old fossil of a dinosaur has been found in Argentina. Scientists from the University of San Juan found the remains in rocks by a river.

The fossil is of a dinosaur called Herrerasaurus. It was a meat-eater standing over two metres tall. It would have looked a bit like Tyrannosaurus Rex, but was much smaller and lighter.

But like the Tyrannosaurus, it is thought to have hunted for animals on its hind legs.

The dinosaur fossil is not the first of this type to be found. But it is by far the most complete.

Palaeontologists say that the find gives a very clear picture of what early dinosaurs were like.

Dog Suspected of Burning Down the House

Try telling Ray Hobley a dog's a man's best friend. After coming home one evening, he found his house in West Bromwich had burned down. Firemen who tackled the blaze believe it was the fault of Mr Hobley's dog, Sam, who chewed a box of matches prior to the accident.

So Pigs Really Can Fly!

A pig being taken to slaughter in Newton Stewart, Dumfries and Galloway, escaped from a horse box through a small gap at the top of the 6ft high tailgate. He was found walking unscathed along the road. Owners Catherine and Peter Makepeace of Wigtown, south-west Scotland have called him Houdini (after the escapologist) and will keep him as a pet.

The Three Cats

Stanley Cook

Three cats share the house – Ebony, Oscar and Susie.

Ebony is a cat who walks by herself. If you try to stroke her, she dodges and runs away. In summer she hides among the plants beneath the lilac tree, like a tiger in ambush. In winter, if you leave the door to the stairs open for one moment, Ebony disappears. You can be sure she has run upstairs and snuggled down among the bedclothes. Her name suits her, for she is as black as ebony all over.

Oscar is a friendly cat who comes out into the road to meet you, especially if it is time to be fed. He loves to be stroked and as you stroke him you can hear him purring with pleasure, as if a little motor were running inside him. But his best friend could not deny that he is a greedy cat. Sometimes even before he has finished his own food, he will try to push Ebony away from her dish and eat her food. He has beautiful ginger fur – he is a smart cat.

Susie is the biggest of the three and she is a clever cat. She can reach up to the door handles, pull them down and open the doors. One day she climbed into the chimney. She didn't like it one bit when she had to be pulled down by her tail. Another time she opened the cooker and ate the chicken inside. Once she opened the pantry door and ate the icing on a birthday cake. When the attic window was left open she climbed out onto the roof and slid down into the gutter. There she stuck and refused to move. Then, when we had got a ladder and were about to rescue her, she went back up the roof, in at the window and back downstairs. When we went inside, there she was, calmly eating her food.

Every day that passes, Ebony hides, Oscar eats, and Susie gets up to one of her tricks.

Acknowledgements

The editor and publisher are grateful for permission to reproduce the following copyright material. All items marked © 1994 are reprinted by permission of the author unless otherwise indicated.

Stanley Cook, 'The Three Cats' © Stanley Cook 1994, reprinted by permission of Sarah Matthews. Pie Corbett, 'Messages' © Pie Corbett 1994. Gina Douthwaite, 'Recipe for Making Better' © Gina Douthwaite 1994. *Early Times,* 'Dinosaur Author', Issue 102, 1990; 'A Fossil Finding', Issue 98, 1989; 'Dog Suspected of Burning Down the House', 'Rude Awakening', 'So Pigs Really Can Fly', Issue 200, 1991; all reprinted by permission of *Early Times.* Wes Magee, 'An A–Z of Items Found on the School Roof by the Caretaker', from *The Witch's Brew and Other Poems,* published by Cambridge University Press. © Wes Magee 1989. Reprinted by permission of the author. Robin Mellor, 'Menus' © Robin Mellor 1994. Tony Mitton, 'Milk Notes in Story Street'; 'Travel Posters from Thomas Fox Travel Agents'; 'Mrs Noah's Notebook' © Tony Mitton 1994. Ian Souter, 'Alphabet Shoes' © Ian Souter 1994; 'Our Family's Taking Back Christmas Shopping List', first published in *Christmas* (Scholastic), © Ian Souter 1992. Reprinted by permission of the author. Roger Stevens, 'Forty-Three Ways to be Happy' © Roger Stevens 1994.

The publisher would like to thank the following for permission to reproduce photographs:

Robert P. Carr/Bruce Coleman Ltd. p. 28; Hans Reinhard/Bruce Coleman Ltd. p. 29.

The monochrone painting of the Herrerasaurus by John Sibbick, p. 27, is reproduced by kind permission of the Natural History Museum.

The illustrations are by: Kathy Baxendale pp. 6–7 (handwriting), 11–12 (handwriting), 14–15 (handwriting), 16, 22–25 (handwriting); David Carter, p. 10; Nicky Cornwell pp. 17–19; Adrienne Geoghehan pp. 22–25; Ann Johns/Maggie Mundy Agency pp. 6–7; Peter Lubach pp. 13–15; Graham Round pp. 11–12; Martin Shovel pp. 4–5; Jake Tebbit pp. 20–21; Marc Vyvyan-Jones pp. 8–9; Sharon Williams p. 31.